From Passion to Profit:

A Guide to Building a Successful Mini Consignment Empire

Copyright © 2024 by Jennifer Lynn

All rights reserved. No part of this book may be reproduced, stored in a retrieval system, or transmitted in any form or by any means, electronic, mechanical, photocopying, recording, or otherwise, without the prior written permission of the publisher.

Published by Jennifer Lynn

Jennifer Lynn
316 10th Street
Worthington, MN 56187

ISBN: 9798327270114

Cover design by Jennifer Lynn

Interior layout by Jennifer Lynn

Printed in United States of America

Disclaimer: The information provided in this book is for educational and informational purposes only. While the author has made every effort to ensure the accuracy of the information presented, readers are advised to conduct their own research and consult with professionals before implementing any strategies or practices discussed herein. The author and publisher shall not be held liable for any damages arising from the use of this book.

Table of Contents

Introduction

Chapter 1: Unveiling Your Passion

Chapter 2: Navigating the Consignment Landscape

Chapter 3: Crafting Your Vision and Mission

Chapter 4: Setting the Stage: Location and Layout

Chapter 5: Building Your Inventory Empire

Chapter 6: Pricing for Profit

Chapter 7: Marketing Magic: Attracting Customers

Chapter 8: Providing Stellar Customer Service

Chapter 9: Managing Operations with Finesse

Chapter 10: Growing Your Business Sustainably

Chapter 11: Overcoming Challenges and Adversities

Chapter 12: Cultivating a Thriving Community

Chapter 13: Balancing Passion with Profitability

Conclusion: Empowering Your Consignment Dream

Acknowledgments

About the Author

Introduction:

Welcome to "From Passion to Profit: Creating Your Mini Retail Empire" – your roadmap to entrepreneurial success in the ever changing world of consignment retail.

Starting on the journey of entrepreneurship is a thrilling and rewarding journey, filled with boundless opportunities for growth, fulfillment, and financial success. As you hold this book in your hands, I invite you to embrace the possibilities that lie ahead, and to envision the limitless potential of your dreams.

Within these pages, you'll discover a treasure trove of insights, strategies, and inspiration learned from years of experience in the consignment industry. From the humble beginnings of a passion for consignment to the realization of a thriving business empire, I'll be your guide, sharing with you the lessons I've learned along the way and offering you practical tools to navigate the path to success.

But success isn't just about financial gain or business growth—it's also about personal fulfillment, purpose, and making a positive impact in your community and the world. As you dive into the pages of this book, I encourage you to embrace the journey wholeheartedly, to nurture your passion, and to cultivate a mindset of abundance, resilience, and gratitude.

Remember, you are capable of achieving greatness beyond your wildest dreams. You have the power to shape your destiny, to overcome obstacles, and to turn challenges into triumphs. Believe in yourself, trust in your abilities, and know that every step you take brings you closer to your dreams.

So let us begin this journey together, with optimism, enthusiasm, and a spirit of adventure. Let us celebrate the joys of entrepreneurship, embrace the lessons of failure, and rejoice in the triumphs of success. And above all, let us remember that the greatest achievements are born from passion, fueled by purpose, and guided by a relentless determination to never give up on our dreams.

Here's to your journey from passion to profit—to building a successful consignment empire that not only transforms your life but also enriches the lives of others. May this book be your companion, your mentor, and your source of inspiration as you set forth on this exhilarating adventure.

With warmest regards and deepest wishes for your success,

Jennifer Lynn

Chapter 1: Unveiling Your Passion

Growing up, my own single mother instilled in me the value of thriftiness, resourcefulness and protecting our environment. She had a knack for finding treasures in the most unexpected places, particularly at consignment shops. As my mother bragged about getting our whole summer wardrobe for around $10 she just beamed with excitement and pride. In those moments, I witnessed firsthand how consignment not only saved us money but also reduced waste, a notion that resonated deeply within me.

When I became a mother myself, I naturally followed in my mother's footsteps, turning to consignment to clothe my growing family. It wasn't just about saving a few bucks; it was about making a conscious choice to embrace sustainable living while still looking stylish and put together. There was something magical about scouring the racks and discovering unique pieces that told a story and pieces that breathed new life into our wardrobes without breaking the bank.

But my journey into the world of consignment wasn't solely driven by practicality; it was fueled by passion. You see, before my days of diaper changes and wrestling practices, I was a number cruncher, an accountant by trade and a professional in a local corporation. While the work was stable and the paycheck reliable, something was missing. Deep down, I yearned for more—a greater sense of purpose, a connection to my community, and most importantly, more time with my family.

I always had a strong desire to be my own boss, to chart my own course and be in control of my destiny. The thought of running my own business, of building something from the ground up, ignited a fire within me that refused to be extinguished. But for years, it remained nothing more than a distant dream, overshadowed by the responsibilities of everyday life. As a small-town mother of two rambunctious boys, life always kept me on my toes.

It wasn't until I found myself at a crossroads, juggling the demands of motherhood and the monotony of corporate life, that I realized the time for change had come. I yearned for a career that not only fulfilled me but also allowed me to give back to my community in a meaningful way. And as fate would have it, the answer was right in front of me all along with our local community lacking a consignment shop.

With each passing day, my passion for consignment grew stronger, fueling my determination to turn my dream into reality. I envisioned a warm and welcoming space where families like mine could discover hidden gems and create new memories, all while making a positive impact on the environment. And so, armed with little more than a vision and a whole lot of determination, I took the leap of faith and embarked on a journey of entrepreneurship.

Years later, I am still filled with excitement and anticipation for what lies ahead for me and my business. My journey is not just about starting a business; it's about embracing my passion, living with purpose, and creating a legacy that extends far beyond the walls of my humble storefront. It's about proving to myself and others that with hard work, dedication, and a whole lot of heart, anything is possible.

So, to all the dreamers and believers out there, I say this: never underestimate the power of your passion or your dreams. Let it guide you, inspire you, and fuel your journey towards a brighter tomorrow. It is through our passions and dreams we discover not only who we are but also who we are meant to be. And in that discovery, we find our truest selves—strong, resilient, and utterly unstoppable.

Chapter 2: Navigating the Consignment Landscape

In the beginning as I dove deeper into the consignment world, I quickly realized that understanding the intricacies of the consignment model was crucial to my success. What once seemed like a simple exchange of goods now revealed itself to be a dynamic and multifaceted business model, ripe with opportunity and potential if done right.

At its core, the consignment model is a relationship between consignors and retailers, where consignors entrust their pre-owned items to be sold on their behalf. Unlike traditional retail, where merchants purchase inventory outright, consignment allows for a more flexible and risk-free approach. Consignors retain ownership of their items until they are sold or donated, at which point the retailer takes a percentage of the sale as a commission. This arrangement not only minimizes financial risk for both parties but also fosters a sense of partnership and trust.

But the consignment model is far from one-size-fits-all. Its versatility allows for endless variations and adaptations that suit the needs of different businesses and industries. From clothing and accessories to furniture and artwork, consignment covers a wide range of categories, catering to diverse tastes and preferences. This flexibility is what makes consignment businesses so resilient and adaptable, capable of weathering economic downturns and changing consumer needs and desires.

As I navigated the consignment business model, I came to recognize the many opportunities and potential that lay before me. I was not bound by the constraints of traditional retail. I saw a world of possibilities waiting to be explored. Whether it was tapping into niche markets, diversifying my inventory, or leveraging technology to reach new customers, the consignment model provided me with the tools and resources to carve out my own path to success. Since beginning in 2016 I have added an intense inventory program using unique barcodes for each item and expanding into e-commerce to sell our products all over the United States. Heck these days I even hire a robot (bot) to manage my e-commerce listings.

But navigating the consignment model wasn't just about seizing opportunities; it was also about understanding the key players that shaped the industry. From seasoned consignment veterans to up-and-coming entrepreneurs, the landscape was populated by a diverse array of individuals and businesses, each bringing their own unique perspective and expertise to the table. I am fortunate to have friends, acquaintances and seasoned consignment business owners that are willing to share their stories, policies, software, lessons, mistakes and their future goals that we can work on together.

I learned so much from my fellow consignment retailers, who served as both allies and competitors in the ever-evolving landscape of consignment. While we are offering a service to the same pool of customers, we also shared a common bond and mutual respect for the consignment model. Networking with other consignment professionals allowed me to gain insights, share best practices, and forge valuable partnerships that strengthened my business.

Among the key players in the consignment industry are the consignors. These are individuals who entrust their beloved belongings to me, placing their trust in my ability to find a new home for their items. In my consignment business, only select items are accepted, inventoried and sold. This quality control method also builds trust with my consignors and customers. Building these strong relationships with consignors is essential to my success, as their continued support and loyalty is what fuels my business.

And of course, the customers are the lifeblood of any retail operation. From seasoned bargain hunters to curious first-timers, my customers come from all walks of life, each seeking their own unique treasure or hidden gem. Understanding their needs, preferences, and shopping habits is crucial to delivering an exceptional customer experience and fostering long-term loyalty. This understanding came easy to me because I share many of the same values, interests and goals as my own customers.

In navigating the consignment model, I quickly learned that success wasn't just about making sales; it was about building relationships, fostering community, and embracing the spirit of collaboration. I recognized consignment versatility and potential, and identified the key players that shaped the industry around my community and as far as New York City. I set myself on a path towards building a thriving and sustainable consignment business—one that would not only fulfill my entrepreneurial dreams but also make a positive impact on my community for years to come.

Chapter 3: Crafting Your Vision and Mission

As I embarked on my journey to build a successful consignment business, I knew that clarity of vision and purpose would be my guiding light. Crafting a compelling vision and mission statement wasn't just about setting lofty goals or empty promises; it was about defining the soul of my business, articulating its purpose, and aligning it with my passion for consignment.

The first step in this process was defining my business goals and objectives. I took the time to reflect on what I hoped to achieve with my consignment journey—both personally and professionally. Was it financial success? Community impact? Work-life balance? By setting clear and measurable goals, I was able to chart a course for my business and keep myself accountable along the way.

But beyond the bottom line, I knew that my consignment business needed a deeper sense of purpose that went beyond profits and margins. That's where articulating my unique value proposition came into play. I asked myself: What sets my business apart from the competition? What value do I bring to my customers and consignors? What makes me stand out in a crowded marketplace?

For me, the answer lay in my unwavering passion for consignment and my commitment to sustainability and community engagement. Unlike traditional retail stores, my consignment business isn't just about selling products; it is about fostering a culture of conscious consumption, where customers can shop guilt-free knowing that they are supporting a more sustainable way of shopping while saving money and being able to earn money as well.

But perhaps most importantly, my unique value proposition was rooted in the personalized service and curated experience that I offered my customers. From hand-selecting the finest consignment pieces to providing expert styling advice, I aimed to create a shopping environment that was as welcoming as it was inspiring. I created a place where customers felt valued, empowered, and excited to explore.

With my vision and mission taking shape, the next step was aligning them with my passion for consignment. For me, consignment wasn't just a business opportunity; it was a calling—a chance to share my love for sustainable fashion and secondhand treasures with the world. It was about connecting with like-minded individuals, building a community, and leaving a positive impact on students, families, the community and the planet.

By infusing my vision and mission with my passion, I was able to create a business that felt authentic, purposeful, and deeply meaningful to me. Every decision I made, from selecting inventory to designing the store layout, was guided by this underlying passion, ensuring that every aspect of my business reflected who I was and what I believed in.

In crafting my vision and mission, I discovered the true essence of my business—*a place where passion meets purpose, where sustainability meets style, and where community meets commerce.* And as I embarked on this exhilarating journey of entrepreneurship, I knew that my vision and mission would serve as my guide towards a future filled with success, fulfillment, and endless possibilities.

Chapter 4: Setting the Stage: Location and Layout

Choosing the perfect location for your consignment business is more than just finding a spot on the map—it's about setting the stage for success, creating a space that not only attracts customers but also fosters a sense of community and connection. As I learned firsthand, the right location can make all the difference in the world, shaping the future and growth of your business and opening doors to endless possibilities.

When I first started my consignment journey, I found myself drawn to a quaint storefront on the outskirts of town. To be honest it was the only retail location available that I could afford. It wasn't the most glamorous location, nor was it flooded with foot traffic, but it had a certain charm and character that spoke to me. Plus, with its affordable rent and ample parking, it offered a low-risk entry point into the world of entrepreneurship—a chance to dip my toes into the water without diving headfirst into the deep end.

But as my business began to grow and evolve, so too did my aspirations. I yearned for a location that would not only accommodate my expanding inventory but also elevate the shopping experience for my customers. That's when fate intervened, presenting me with the opportunity to purchase a building downtown—a prime location right in the heart of Worthington's bustling commercial district.

With its central location and vibrant atmosphere, the downtown building was everything I had ever dreamed of and more. It was a place where locals and tourists alike gathered to shop, dine, and socialize—a hub of activity and energy that breathed new life into my business. But more than that, it was a symbol of progress and growth—a testament to how far I had come on my journey from humble beginnings to entrepreneurial success.

With the perfect location secured, the next step was designing an inviting and functional space that would not only attract customers but also cater to the needs of my consignors. I wanted to create an environment that felt like a home away from home—a place where people could escape the hustle and bustle of daily life and lose themselves in the thrill of discovery.

To achieve this, I paid careful attention to every detail of the layout and design, from the placement of racks and shelves to the color scheme and decor. I wanted the space to feel open and airy, with plenty of room for customers to browse and explore at their leisure. At the same time, I needed to ensure that the layout was optimized for efficiency, allowing me to process incoming inventory quickly and seamlessly.

One of the key considerations in designing the layout was maximizing display space to showcase my curated selection of consignment treasures. I invested in high-quality shelving units and display fixtures, arranging them in a way that highlighted the unique features of each item and encouraged customers to linger and explore. By creating visually appealing displays I was able to capture the attention of potential customers and draw them into the world of consignment.

But perhaps the most important aspect of the layout was creating separate areas for customers and consignors, each tailored to their specific needs. For customers, I designed cozy seating areas where they could relax and try on clothes, as well as designated checkout counters for quick and convenient transactions. For consignors, I set up dedicated intake stations where they could drop off their items and discuss pricing and commission details with my staff.

In designing the layout of my consignment space, I strived to strike a balance between form and function, aesthetics and practicality. I wanted to create an environment that was not only visually appealing but also conducive to sales and efficiency—a space where customers felt welcomed and inspired, and consignors felt valued and respected.

As I look back on the evolution of my consignment business, I am reminded of the importance of location and layout in shaping its success. From humble beginnings in a small storefront to the vibrant downtown destination it is today, my consignment space has been more than just a place of business—it has been a reflection of my vision, a manifestation of my passion, and a testament to the power of entrepreneurship to transform lives and communities.

Chapter 5: Building Your Inventory Empire

As my consignment business continued to grow and evolve, so did the challenges and complexities of managing inventory. What had once been a manageable task of keeping records by hand and paper quickly ballooned into a daunting endeavor as the number of consignor accounts multiplied from 150 to 1000. It became increasingly clear that our outdated manual system was no longer sustainable, and we were forced to confront the need for a more sophisticated approach to inventory management.

One of the biggest struggles we faced was the sheer volume of items coming in from consignors on a daily basis. With such a diverse array of merchandise—ranging from clothing and accessories to furniture and home decor—keeping track of everything became a nightmare. Misplaced items, inaccurate records, and missed sales opportunities were all too common occurrences, threatening to undermine the efficiency and profitability of our business.

To address these challenges, we knew that we needed to implement a more robust inventory management system—one that could handle the complexities of our growing inventory and streamline our operations. After much research and deliberation, we made the decision to invest in an access inventory program, which promised to provide us with the tools and capabilities we needed to take our inventory management to the next level.

The transition to the access inventory program was not without its challenges. It required us to digitize our entire inventory catalog, inputting each item into the system manually—a tedious and time-consuming process that tested our patience and productivity. But despite the initial hurdles, we soon began to reap the benefits of our new inventory management system.

With the access inventory program in place, we were able to track incoming and outgoing inventory more accurately and efficiently than ever before. Consignor accounts were seamlessly integrated into the system, allowing us to keep track of each individual's items, sales, and commissions with ease. Automated alerts and reminders helped us stay on top of inventory deadlines and pricing updates, ensuring that nothing fell through the cracks.

But perhaps the most transformative aspect of the access inventory program was its reporting capabilities. With just a few clicks, we could generate detailed reports on sales trends, inventory turnover, and consignor performance, providing us with valuable insights that informed our business decisions and strategies. Armed with this data-driven approach, we were able to curate a more diverse and desirable inventory mix, catering to the evolving needs and desires of our customers.

But just as we were beginning to reap the rewards of our investment in the access inventory program, the world was thrown into chaos by the onset of the global pandemic in 2020. Overnight, our business was turned upside down as lockdowns and social distancing measures forced us to close our doors and rethink our approach to inventory management once again.

In the face of unprecedented challenges, we knew that we needed to adapt quickly in order to survive. It was at this time we implemented a cloud based inventory and point of sale system where we were able to pivot to online sales and curbside pickup, allowing us to continue serving our customers and generating revenue even in the midst of uncertainty. And as the world slowly began to reopen, we emerged stronger and more resilient than ever before, armed with the knowledge and experience gained from our journey through the trials and tribulations of inventory management in the digital age.

As our inventory management, point of sale and e-commerce capabilities improved, so did our relationships with consignors and customers. As a result we increased our consignment accounts and we were able to weather the retail downturn in 2020. With accurate and up-to-date records at our fingertips, we were able to provide consignors with greater transparency and accountability, building trust and confidence in our business practices. At the same time, we were able to offer more sale opportunities of our consigned items by selling online and shipping all over the United States.

Chapter 6: Pricing for Profit

In the world of consignment, pricing is both an art and a science—a delicate balancing act that requires careful consideration of various factors, from market trends and item condition to customer expectations and business objectives. For my consignment business in Worthington, Minnesota, pricing wasn't just about turning a profit; it was about fulfilling a larger mission—to provide families with everything they needed for their homes and clothing, all while keeping them within reach of their budgets and without resorting to big-box retailers or out-of-town shopping trips.

Mastering the art of pricing consignment items was no easy feat. It required a deep understanding of the market and a keen eye for value—a knack for recognizing the worth of each item and pricing it accordingly. But it also demanded flexibility and adaptability, as pricing strategies needed to evolve in response to changing trends and customer demand.

One of the guiding principles of our pricing strategy was to balance competitiveness with profitability. While we wanted to offer competitive prices that would attract customers and keep them coming back, we also needed to ensure that our prices were set at a level that would allow us to cover our costs and generate a reasonable profit margin. It was a delicate dance, requiring us to strike the right balance between affordability and sustainability.

To achieve this balance, we employed a variety of pricing techniques, ranging from cost-based pricing to value-based pricing. For items with clear market value, such as designer clothing or high-end furniture, we used a value-based approach, pricing them based on their perceived worth and desirability. For items with less clear market value, such as generic household goods or everyday clothing, we relied on cost-based pricing, taking into account factors such as condition, brand, and demand.

But pricing wasn't just about setting numbers; it was also about tapping into the psychology of consumer behavior to drive sales. We leveraged pricing strategies such as bundling, discounting, and tiered pricing to provide incentives for purchases and maximize revenue. By offering special promotions and discounts on certain items, we were able to create a sense of urgency and excitement among customers, encouraging them to take advantage of the deals while they lasted.

At the same time, we were mindful of the importance of transparency and consistency in pricing. We made sure that our pricing was clear and upfront, with no hidden fees or surprises at checkout. We also strived to maintain consistency in pricing across different categories and items, ensuring that customers could trust us to offer fair and competitive prices every time they visited our store.

Ultimately, our pricing strategy was guided by a simple yet powerful principle—to provide families with the goods they needed at prices they could afford, all while ensuring the long-term sustainability and profitability of our business. By mastering the art and science of pricing consignment items and using a standard 40% Consignor and 60% Business Split, we were able to fulfill our mission of serving our community and building a business that would endure for years to come.

Chapter 7: Marketing Magic: Attracting Customers

In the world of consignment, attracting customers isn't just about offering great products—it's about creating a buzz, building a community, and engaging with your audience in meaningful ways. As the owner of a consignment business in Worthington, Minnesota, I quickly learned that effective marketing was the key to driving traffic to my store and keeping customers coming back for more. From word of mouth to social media, newspapers, radio, email, flyers and text marketing, I've tried it all, constantly adapting my approach to meet the needs of my target audience.

Developing a comprehensive marketing plan tailored to your target audience is essential for success. For me, this meant understanding the demographics and preferences of my customers—families looking for affordable, sustainable options for their homes and clothing—and tailoring my marketing efforts to resonate with them. I focused on creating messaging that emphasized the value and convenience of consignment shopping, highlighting the benefits of finding quality items that are at unbeatable prices.

Harnessing the power of digital marketing channels was another crucial component of my marketing strategy. In today's digital age, having a strong online presence is essential for reaching customers where they spend the majority of their time. I invested time and resources into building a website and cultivating a vibrant presence on social media platforms like Facebook, Instagram, and Pinterest. Through engaging content, eye-catching visuals, and targeted advertising, I was able to connect with my audience on a deeper level and drive traffic to my store.

But digital marketing was just one piece of the puzzle. I also recognized the importance of offline marketing tactics, such as hanging up flyers and networking daily. Word of mouth has always been one of the most powerful forms of advertising for my business, with satisfied customers recommending us to their friends and family. By providing exceptional service and creating memorable shopping experiences, I was able to turn customers into brand ambassadors, spreading the word about my business far and wide.

In addition to traditional and digital marketing channels, I recently began exploring the world of text marketing as a way to further engage with my customers and drive sales. By sending personalized text messages with exclusive offers, promotions, and event invitations, I'm able to connect with customers in real-time and provide incentives to visit my store or shop online.

Implementing creative promotional strategies has been another key element of my marketing success. From hosting special events and themed sales to offering loyalty programs and referral incentives, I'm always looking for new ways to boost visibility and drive sales. By thinking outside the box and surprising my customers with unique promotions and experiences, I'm able to stand out and keep them coming back for more.

In the end, marketing magic isn't about flashy gimmicks or big-budget campaigns—it's about understanding your audience, meeting their needs, and building meaningful relationships that keep them coming back for more. By developing a comprehensive marketing plan tailored to my target audience, harnessing the power of digital marketing channels, and implementing creative promotional strategies, I've been able to attract customers, drive sales, and build a thriving consignment business that continues to grow and evolve with each passing day.

Chapter 8: Providing Stellar Customer Service

In the world of consignment, exceptional customer service isn't just a nice-to-have—it's a cornerstone of success. As the owner of a consignment business, I've always believed that happy customers are the foundation of my business. That's why I've made it my mission to provide stellar customer service that not only meets but exceeds their expectations every step of the way.

Creating memorable customer experiences is at the heart of what we do. From the moment a customer walks through the door, we strive to make them feel welcome, valued, and appreciated. We greet them with a warm smile, offer assistance if needed, and go out of our way to ensure that their shopping experience is nothing short of extraordinary.

One of the keys to providing exceptional customer service is listening to our customers and responding to their needs and preferences. We take the time to get to know them on a personal level, asking questions, listening to their feedback, and tailoring our recommendations to their individual tastes and preferences. Whether they're looking for a specific item or just browsing for inspiration, we're always ready to lend a helping hand and provide guidance and advice.

But exceptional customer service isn't just about being friendly and helpful—it's also about handling inquiries, feedback, and complaints with professionalism and empathy. We understand that mistakes happen, and when they do, we own up to them and take swift action to make things right. Whether it's a pricing error, a damaged item, or a misunderstanding, we always strive to resolve issues quickly and to the customer's satisfaction.

In addition to handling inquiries and complaints, we also actively seek out feedback from our customers to continually improve our service and offerings. We encourage them to share their thoughts and suggestions with us, whether it's in person, through email, or via social media. By listening to their feedback and taking it to heart, we're able to identify areas for improvement and make necessary adjustments to better serve our customers.

But providing exceptional customer service isn't just about meeting expectations—it's about going above and beyond to exceed them. Whether it's offering personalized styling advice, providing complimentary gift wrapping, or remembering a customer's special event, we're always looking for ways to surprise and delight our customers and make them feel special.

One of the most rewarding aspects of providing exceptional customer service is seeing the impact it has on our customers' lives. We've had customers come to us in search of a specific item for a special occasion, only to leave with a smile on their face and a newfound sense of confidence and satisfaction. Knowing that we've made a positive difference in their lives is what drives us to continually raise the bar and strive for excellence in everything we do.

In the end, providing exceptional customer service isn't just about making sales—it's about building meaningful relationships, fostering loyalty, and creating memorable experiences that keep customers coming back time and time again. By creating memorable customer experiences, handling inquiries and feedback with professionalism and empathy, and going above and beyond to exceed customer expectations, we've been able to build a loyal customer base and establish ourselves as a trusted destination for consignment shopping in our community and online.

Chapter 9: Managing Operations with Finesse

Efficiency and precision are the backbone of any successful consignment business. As the owner of a thriving consignment store in Worthington, Minnesota, I've learned firsthand the importance of establishing efficient processes, efficient record keeping and operation systems that can be copied and repeated by staff is the key to manage operations with finesse. From receiving and inspecting inventory to merchandising and administrative tasks, every aspect of our operations is meticulously planned, understood/taught and executed to ensure maximum productivity and customer satisfaction.

At the heart of our operations is our process for receiving, inspecting, and merchandising inventory. We've established strict guidelines for consignors, requiring all items to be brought in a tote, freshly cleaned, and in working and undamaged condition. Quality control is non-negotiable—we are highly selective about the items we choose to resell in our store, ensuring that only the highest quality merchandise makes it onto our shelves or sales floor.

Upon arrival, each item is meticulously inspected for signs of wear, damage, or defects. Our trained staff carefully assesses the condition of each item, checking for any imperfections that may affect its resale value or appeal to customers. Items that meet our strict quality standards are then inventoried, tagged and photographed. When entered into our inventory system each item is assigned a unique barcode that tracks its journey from inventory to customer sale and beyond.

Speaking of our new inventory tracking system, it has been instrumental in streamlining our operations and optimizing productivity since 2020. By leveraging cloud-based technology, we're able to access real-time inventory data from anywhere, at any time, allowing us to keep track of stock levels, monitor sales trends, and make informed decisions on the fly. The system also automates many administrative tasks, such as generating sales reports, tracking consignor payouts, and managing returns, saving us time and resources that can be better spent on other aspects of our business.

But perhaps the most significant impact of our inventory system is its ability to enhance the customer experience. With accurate and up-to-date inventory information at our fingertips, we're able to provide customers with the assurance that the items they see online or in-store are available for purchase. This reduces the risk of disappointment and frustration, helping to build trust and loyalty among our customer base in-store and online.

In conclusion, managing operations with finesse is essential for the success of any consignment business. By establishing efficient processes for receiving, inspecting, and merchandising inventory, implementing a robust inventory tracking or management systems and streamlining administrative tasks, we're able to optimize productivity, enhance the customer experience, and position ourselves for long-term success in the competitive world of consignment retail.

Chapter 10: Growing Your Business Sustainably

Expanding a consignment business can be both exhilarating and daunting, but when opportunities arise, seizing them can lead to remarkable growth and success. In 2022, we took a bold step forward by opening a second location in my hometown of Windom, Minnesota, despite it being a half hour away from our original store in Worthington. It was an opportunity we couldn't pass up, especially considering the closure of numerous consignment and retail clothing businesses in Windom. This move not only expanded our reach but also allowed us to fill a void in the local market and serve a new community.

Also adding a Vintage Boutique to our first location was a strategic decision to diversify our inventory and appeal to a broader customer base. Vintage clothing and accessories have seen a resurgence in popularity in recent years, and we wanted to capitalize on this trend by offering unique, one-of-a-kind pieces that set us apart from the competition. By curating a selection of vintage treasures alongside our consignment items, we were able to attract a new demographic of customers and further establish ourselves as a destination for fashion-forward shoppers.

In addition to expanding our physical presence, we also recognized the importance of diversifying our revenue streams and product offerings to ensure long-term sustainability. One way we achieved this was through our clearing house service, which allowed retail stores to liquidate their excess inventory through our consignment channels. This not only provided us with a steady stream of high-quality merchandise but also helped struggling businesses recoup losses and avoid waste—a win-win for everyone involved.

But perhaps the most significant expansion for our business came in the form of online sales. With the rise of e-commerce platforms and the shift towards online shopping, we knew that we needed to meet our customers where they were—online. We invested in building a robust e-commerce website and established a presence on various online marketplaces, allowing us to reach customers beyond the confines of our physical locations and expand our market reach exponentially.

However, growth isn't just about adding new locations or product lines—it's also about fostering a culture of innovation and adaptability. In an ever-changing industry, we understand the importance of staying ahead of the curve and constantly evolving to meet the needs and preferences of our customers. Whether it's embracing new technologies, experimenting with innovative marketing strategies, or pivoting in response to changing market conditions, we're always looking for ways to stay relevant and competitive in a rapidly evolving landscape.

In conclusion, growing your business' sustainability requires a strategic approach that balances expansion with diversification, innovation, and adaptability. By exploring expansion opportunities and growth strategies, diversifying revenue streams and product offerings, and fostering a culture of innovation and adaptability, we've been able to position our consignment business for long-term success and continued growth in the dynamic and ever-changing retail landscape.

Chapter 11: Overcoming Challenges and Adversities

In the seven years since I embarked on my journey as a consignment business owner, I've faced more than my fair share of challenges and adversities. From the highs of growth and success to the lows of hardship and loss, my path has been marked by trials and tribulations that have tested my resilience, strength, and determination. But through it all, I've learned invaluable lessons about perseverance, adaptability, and the power of seeking help and support when times get tough.

Anticipating and navigating common pitfalls in the consignment industry is no easy task, but it's essential for long-term success. From fluctuating market trends and economic downturns to inventory management issues and customer satisfaction concerns, there are countless challenges that consignment business owners may encounter along the way. By staying vigilant, staying informed, and staying one step ahead of potential pitfalls, I've been able to navigate these challenges with grace and resilience.

Developing resilience and problem-solving skills has been key to overcoming the many obstacles I've faced on my journey. When adversity strikes, it's easy to feel overwhelmed and defeated, but I've learned to approach challenges with a positive mindset and a determination to find solutions. Whether it's finding creative ways to boost sales during a slow season or adapting our operations to meet the demands of a global pandemic, I've always been willing to roll up my sleeves and do whatever it takes to keep my business moving forward.

But perhaps the most important lesson I've learned is the power of seeking support and guidance from mentors and peers. No one can navigate the ups and downs of entrepreneurship alone, and having a strong support network can make all the difference in the world. Over the years, I've been fortunate to connect with fellow business owners, industry experts, and mentors who have offered invaluable advice, encouragement, and perspective when I needed it the most.

Whether it's attending networking events, joining industry associations, or seeking out one-on-one mentorship opportunities, I've never been afraid to reach out and ask for help when I needed it. And in doing so, I've built a network of support that has helped me weather even the toughest storms and emerge stronger and more resilient on the other side.

In conclusion, overcoming challenges and adversities is an inevitable part of the entrepreneurial journey, but it's also an opportunity for growth, learning, and personal development. By anticipating and navigating common pitfalls in the consignment industry, developing resilience and problem-solving skills, and seeking support and guidance from mentors and peers, I've been able to overcome obstacles, achieve success, and continue pursuing my passion for consignment with renewed perspectives, strength and determination.

Chapter 12: Cultivating a Thriving Community

As I reflect on the journey of my consignment business—a journey marked by growth, challenges, and countless lessons learned—I am filled with gratitude for the achievements and milestones that have shaped my path. From humble beginnings to the thriving enterprise it is today, my business has been a labor of love—a testament to the power of passion, purpose, and perseverance.

But success is not measured solely by financial gain or business growth—it is also defined by the impact we have on others and the communities we serve. That's why, as I continue on this journey, I am committed to cultivating a thriving community—one where people feel connected, supported, and empowered to pursue their dreams and aspirations.

Engaging with local communities and stakeholders has always been a priority for me. From the very beginning, I've sought to build strong relationships with customers, consignors, and fellow business owners, recognizing that collaboration and cooperation are essential for collective success. By actively participating in community events, attending local meetings, and supporting neighborhood initiatives, I've been able to foster a sense of belonging and camaraderie that extends far beyond the walls of my store.

But cultivating a thriving community isn't just about forging connections—it's also about giving back and supporting charitable initiatives that make a positive impact on the lives of others. Whether it's donating clothing and household items to families in need, sponsoring local charities and fundraisers, or volunteering my time and expertise to support community organizations, I am committed to using my business as a force for good and making a meaningful difference in the world around me.

Celebrating milestones is an important part of cultivating a thriving community. Whether it's the anniversary of my business, the opening of a new location, or the achievement of a personal goal, I believe in taking the time to acknowledge and celebrate the achievements and successes of myself, my team, and my community. By recognizing and honoring these milestones, we not only inspire others to reach for their own dreams but also create lasting memories and connections that strengthen the bonds of our community.

As the journey continues for me, I am more committed than ever to paying my success forward in my community, industry, and among fellow business owners. Whether it's sharing my knowledge and experience through mentorship and coaching, advocating for policies and initiatives that support small businesses, or simply lending a helping hand to those in need, I am determined to make a positive impact and leave a lasting legacy that extends far beyond the confines of my business.

In conclusion, cultivating a thriving community is not just a goal—it's a way of life. By engaging with local communities and stakeholders, supporting charitable initiatives and community events, and building meaningful connections that foster loyalty and trust, I am committed to creating a world where everyone has the opportunity to thrive and succeed. And as the journey continues, I will always look for ways to sustain my passion, purpose, and legacy in my business, ensuring that future generations can benefit from the seeds of success that we sow today.

Chapter 13: Balancing Passion with Profitability

In the dynamic world of entrepreneurship, finding the delicate balance between passion and profitability is essential for long-term success. As a consignment business owner, I've learned firsthand the importance of pursuing my passion while also maintaining a keen eye on the bottom line. In Chapter 13, we explore the art of striking a harmonious balance between personal fulfillment and financial success.

Setting realistic goals (while reaching beyond the stars) and benchmarks for growth is the cornerstone of balancing passion with profitability. When I started my consignment business, I had a vision—a dream of creating a thriving community hub where families could find quality items at affordable prices. But I also knew that in order to turn that vision into reality, I needed to set clear, actionable goals and benchmarks for growth.

Setting realistic goals is about understanding my strengths, limitations, and the resources at my disposal. It's about breaking down my larger vision into smaller, achievable milestones that I can work towards each day, week, and month. Whether it's increasing sales by a certain percentage, expanding into a new market, or improving operational efficiency, setting realistic goals allows me to stay focused, motivated, and on track towards realizing my vision.

But while setting realistic goals is important, so too is reaching beyond the stars and pushing the boundaries of what's possible. As an entrepreneur, I've always believed in dreaming big and aiming high. I refuse to settle for mediocrity or complacency—I'm constantly challenging myself to think outside the box, take calculated risks, and pursue ambitious goals that push me out of my comfort zone.

Celebrating achievements and milestones along the journey is crucial for maintaining motivation and momentum. In the fast-paced world of entrepreneurship, it's easy to get caught up in the daily grind and lose sight of how far we've come. But by taking the time to pause, reflect, and celebrate our achievements, we're able to acknowledge the hard work and dedication that has brought us to where we are today.

Whether it's reaching a sales milestone, opening a new location, or receiving recognition for our contributions to the community, celebrating achievements is an opportunity to express gratitude, share success with others, and recharge our batteries for the journey ahead. It's a reminder that every step forward, no matter how small, brings us closer to our ultimate goal of success and fulfillment.

In conclusion, balancing passion with profitability is a delicate dance—one that requires us to set realistic goals, reach beyond the stars, and celebrate achievements along the journey. By staying true to our passion, while also keeping a sharp focus on profitability, we're able to create a business that not only brings us personal fulfillment but also generates sustainable financial success for years to come. And as the journey continues, I'm excited to see where passion and profitability will take me next

Conclusion: Empowering Your Consignment Dream

As we come to the end of our journey in this book, it's a moment to pause and reflect on the lessons learned, the insights gained, and the endless possibilities that lie ahead. From the humble beginnings of a dream to the realization of a thriving business, this book serves as a roadmap for turning passion into profit and building a sustainable empire in the consignment industry.

Reflecting on your journey from passion to profit, you've overcome obstacles, seized opportunities, and transformed challenges into triumphs. You've embraced the unique blend of creativity, resourcefulness, and resilience that defines the consignment business, and you've emerged stronger and more determined than ever to pursue your dreams with passion and purpose.

Along the way, you've learned key insights and strategies that have guided your path to success. From crafting a compelling vision and mission to curating a diverse and desirable inventory mix, from mastering the art and science of pricing to harnessing the power of marketing and customer service, you've honed your skills and expertise to build a business that stands apart from the rest.

But the journey doesn't end here—it's only just beginning. As you look ahead to building a thriving and sustainable consignment empire, you're filled with excitement, anticipation, and a sense of possibility. You see endless opportunities for growth, innovation, and impact, and you're ready to seize them with gusto.

Implementing actionable takeaways from Passion to Profit, you're poised to take your business to new heights. Whether it's expanding into new markets, diversifying revenue streams, or embracing emerging technologies, you're committed to staying ahead of the curve and pushing the boundaries of what's possible in the consignment industry.

But perhaps most importantly, you're inspired to empower others to embark on their own entrepreneurial ventures with passion and purpose. You understand the transformative power of entrepreneurship—the ability to create something from nothing, to turn dreams into reality, and to make a positive impact on the world around you.

As you continue on your journey, remember that the sky's the limit. With passion as your fuel and purpose as your compass, there's no telling what you can achieve. So go forth with confidence, courage, and conviction, and let your consignment dream soar to new heights of success and fulfillment.

Acknowledgements

I am forever grateful to my partner, whose love, support, and encouragement have been a constant source of inspiration throughout my journey. Your belief in me has fueled my determination.

To my mother & father(s), whose guidance and mentorship has been invaluable to me. Your insights have helped me navigate the challenges of parenthood & entrepreneurship.

I am blessed by my immediate family for their help, love and understanding, especially during the long hours and late nights spent building my business. Your patience, sacrifice, and unwavering belief in me have been the foundation of my success.

I am deeply indebted to my close business friends & our community for its generosity and spirit of collaboration. From local business owners to loyal customers, your support has been instrumental in shaping the success of my consignment business. I am proud to be a part of a vibrant and thriving community.

Last but certainly not least, I want to thank my children for being my greatest motivation and inspiration. Your boundless energy, creativity, and love reminds me every day of what truly matters in life. I am grateful for the support, joy and laughter you bring into my world, and I am honored to be your parent.

To all those who have played a part in my journey, whether big or small, I offer my heartfelt thank you. Your contributions have not gone unnoticed, and I am forever grateful for your presence in my life.

With deepest appreciation,

Jennifer Lynn

About the Author

Jennifer Lynn is a dynamic entrepreneur, visionary leader, and passionate advocate for sustainable business practices. With over seven years of experience in the consignment industry, she has established herself as an expert in the field, renowned for her innovative approach and unwavering commitment to excellence.

Driven by a deep-seated passion for entrepreneurship and a desire to create positive change in her community, Jennifer Lynn embarked on her journey into the consignment business with a clear vision: to build a thriving empire that not only delivers financial success but also makes a meaningful difference in the lives of others.

Throughout her career, Jennifer Lynn has demonstrated a remarkable ability to adapt to changing market trends, embrace new technologies, and anticipate the evolving needs of her customers. By combining her keen business insight with a genuine passion for sustainability and community engagement, she has successfully positioned her business as a leader in her industry.

Beyond her entrepreneurial pursuits, Jennifer Lynn is deeply committed to giving back to the community and fostering a culture of generosity and compassion. She has actively supported charitable initiatives, volunteered her time and resources to local causes, and serves as a mentor and inspiration to aspiring entrepreneurs.

With a relentless drive for success, an unwavering dedication to excellence, and a profound belief in the power of entrepreneurship to bring about positive change, Jennifer Lynn continues to inspire and empower others to pursue their dreams and build a better world for future generations. Through her leadership, her passion for consignment has evolved into a thriving business empire, leaving an unforgettable mark on the industry and the community alike.

Notes / Ideas / Inspirations

Notes / Ideas / Inspirations

Notes / Ideas / Inspirations

Notes / Ideas / Inspirations

Notes / Ideas / Inspirations

Notes / Ideas / Inspirations

Notes / Ideas / Inspirations

Notes / Ideas / Inspirations

Notes / Ideas / Inspirations

Notes / Ideas / Inspirations

Notes / Ideas / Inspirations

Notes / Ideas / Inspirations

Notes / Ideas / Inspirations

Notes / Ideas / Inspirations

Notes / Ideas / Inspirations

See my Team in action:

www.threadsanddecor.com

www.facebook.com/threadsanddecor

www.facebook.com/threadsanddecor-windom

www.poshmark.com/closet/jsolt2

www.instagram.com/threads_and_decor

www.pinterest.com/threadsanddecor

www.ingramcontent.com/pod-product-compliance
Lightning Source LLC
Chambersburg PA
CBHW030451220526
45464CB00006B/2485